T0020226

PEOPLE YOU
SHOULD KNOW

MALCOLM X

Get to Know the Civil Rights Activist

by Ebony Joy Wilkins

Consultant: Ricardo Guthrie, PhD
Director and Associate Professor, Ethnic Studies
Northern Arizona University

CAPSTONE PRESS
a capstone imprint

Fact Finders Books are published by Capstone Press, an imprint of Capstone.
1710 Roe Crest Drive, North Mankato, Minnesota 56003
www.capstonepub.com

Library of Congress Cataloging-in-Publication Data is available on the Library of Congress website.
ISBN 978-1-5435-9091-3 (library binding)
ISBN 978-1-4966-6579-9 (paperback)
ISBN 978-1-5435-9092-0 (eBook PDF)

Summary: Malcolm X is known as a leader of the civil rights movement. He faced racism, spent time in prison, became a minister, joined the Nation of Islam, left, took a pilgrimage to Mecca, traveled the world, and became a public figure before his assassination. Explore how his words shaped the civil rights movement and the people who called him a leader.

Photo Credits
Alamy: ClassicStock, 16, Everett Collection, 9, Sueddeutsche Zeitung Photo, 14; AP Photo: Bill Chaplis, 20; Getty Images: Bettmann, cover, 22, Hulton Archive/Bob Parent, 26, Pictorial Parade, 5, The LIFE Picture Collection/Hansel Mieth, 19; Library of Congress: 10, 29; Newscom: Pictures From History, 24; Shutterstock: Everett Historical, 13, Syok2aje, 6

Design Elements by Shutterstock

Editorial Credits
Mari Bolte, editor; Dina Her, designer; Svetlana Zhurkin, media researcher; Tori Abraham, production specialist

Source Notes
page 6, line 10: Mayor's Office on African American Affairs. https://moaaa.dc.gov/page/malcolm-x. Accessed May 1, 2019.
page 15, line 8: X, Malcolm. *The Autobiography of Malcolm X, with the Assistance of Alex Haley.* New York: Grove Press, 1966, page 3.
page 19, line 19: ibid., page 38.
page 19, line 23: ibid.
page 25, line 13: ibid., page 258.
page 27, line 11: Malcolm X Biography. https://www.malcolmx.com/biography/. Accessed May 13, 2019.
page 29, photo caption: *Malcolm X*, page 2.

All internet sites appearing in back matter were available and accurate when this book was sent to press.

TABLE OF CONTENTS

A NATURAL-BORN LEADER

Malcolm X stepped off a plane and onto the soil of Saudi Arabia in 1964. The holy city of Mecca was already filled with thousands of other Muslims. They were all there on a **Hajj** journey. This journey was a once-in-a-lifetime opportunity for a Muslim. Malcolm decided to travel from the United States to the holy city to pray about a new direction his life was taking.

Malcolm had preached the words of the Nation of **Islam** (NOI) for years. But recently, he and the organization had parted ways. It was time for Malcolm to rethink his feelings on race and religion in America.

Black nationalism—the support or awareness for, and unity and independence of, Black people in a country

Hajj—a religious journey to the holy city of Mecca, Saudi Arabia

Islam—a religion founded on the Arabian Peninsula in the seventh century by the Prophet Muhammad

The Nation of Islam

Founded in 1930 by W. D. Fard, the Nation of Islam (NOI) combined elements of the Islamic religion and **Black nationalism** in the United States. A man named Elijah Muhammad led the group until 1975. His leadership grew the NOI from a small group in Detroit, Michigan, to an organization with financial investments across the country.

Muhammad preached that the NOI's goal was to establish a separate nation for Black people. He encouraged his followers to reject the names given to them by the enslaver of their enslaved ancestors and take Muslim names instead, as he, formerly Elijah Poole, had. Malcolm chose to shed his last name of "Little" and replaced it with "X." The X signified that his true name had been lost to slavery.

Malcolm met with Saudi Arabia's King Faisal during his Hajj in 1964.

All his life, Malcolm had judged people based on the color of their skin. He had spoken against "White devils" and supported the independence of Black people in the United States. But in Mecca, near North Africa and the Middle East, Malcolm was able to hear thoughts and beliefs from people of many different cultures. He realized that the color of people's skin didn't matter—their intentions did. "Power in defense of freedom is greater than power in behalf of tyranny and oppression," he said. "Because power, real power, comes from our conviction which produces action, uncompromising action."

All Muslims who are physically and financially able are expected to make a Hajj during their lifetimes. The Ka'aba, shown here, is located inside the Grand Mosque in Mecca.

Malcolm changed his views on race and religion after his Hajj in 1964. He began to follow Sunni Islam, a traditional branch of the faith. He adopted the new name of El-Hajj Malik El-Shabazz. His new message promoted peace, unity, and equal rights for all people. He welcomed the idea that **human rights** were for everyone. Malcolm X was a new man.

The Hajj

The Hajj is an annual pilgrimage to Mecca. It is made during the last month of the Muslim calendar. While in Mecca, Muslims follow in the footsteps of Prophet Ibrahim and circle the Ka'aba—"the house of God"—seven times, stop by the neighborhood of Mina to read the Quran, pray in the Arafat valley, pick up 49 rocks at Muzdalifah, throw the rocks at three pillars, and circle the Ka'aba seven more times in Mecca. Muslims are expected to make the journey at least once in their lifetimes. Millions make the trip each year.

human rights—the idea that all people should be treated fairly

2 ▸ BROTHERHOOD IS A TWO-WAY STREET

Earl and Louise Norton Little knew they would have their hands full when Malcolm was born on May 19, 1925. The fourth of eight children, he was curious about the world around him.

Georgia-native Earl was a Baptist minister. Louise was an **activist**. The two met while working for Marcus Garvey's Universal Negro Improvement Association (UNIA). The UNIA focused on Black racial pride and economic advancement.

activist—a person who works for social or political change

civil rights—the rights that all people have to freedom and equal treatment under the law

race leader—an activist who unites people on the basis of shared racial, cultural, and historical beliefs

In 1920, five years before Malcolm was born, the UNIA held its first convention in New York City. More than 25,000 people attended a speech given by Marcus Garvey.

The family moved a lot. Malcolm was born in Omaha, Nebraska. Before he turned 6 years old, they lived in Milwaukee, Wisconsin; East Chicago, Indiana; and finally, Lansing, Michigan. Earl traveled among area congregations as a visiting preacher. It was his dream to own a home, grow his own food, and open a store.

DID YOU KNOW?

Louise Norton Little was born in Grenada, West Indies. She never met her father, who was White. Malcolm was born with freckles and reddish-brown hair. He struggled with his identity as a Black man during much of his life.

Marcus Garvey

Marcus Garvey (1887–1940) was a **race leader** and early **civil rights** advocate. He believed in uplifting people of African descent. He founded a Black newspaper, a Black shipping company, and the UNIA in the 1920s.

Laws called Black Codes, first passed in 1865, were the first move toward segregation. Even the most basic things, such as water fountains, were segregated.

A (Brief) History of Inequality in America

Enslaved Africans had been brought to the Americas since the early 1500s. At the time of the Civil War (1861–1865), more than 4 million people were enslaved. Most of those people were of African descent. In 1861, thirteen states in the South **seceded** from the United States and made their own government. These states supported slavery, while most Northern states had banned the practice.

After the Civil War ended, the United States government added **amendments** to the Constitution.

- The 13th Amendment, passed in 1865, formally ended slavery in the United States.

- The 14th Amendment, passed in 1868, defined a citizen as any person born or naturalized in the United States.

- The 15th Amendment, passed in 1870, said the U.S. government could not deny the right to vote based on race, color, or past enslavement.

But in the late 1870s, politicians in the South passed and enforced **Jim Crow segregation**. Black people were denied equal access to quality schools, swimming pools, libraries, theaters, restaurants, hospitals, and public transportation.

Jim Crow laws denied Black people the right to vote and to own land. For example, people who could not read or did not own property could vote only if their fathers or grandfathers had voted. But since many Black people had fathers or grandfathers who had been enslaved, this only benefited landowning White people.

Later acts of government helped, at least legally. The Voting Rights Act of 1965 ended laws that prevented Black people from voting. *Loving v. Virginia* in 1967 ended all laws banning interracial marriage. The Fair Housing Act of 1968 banned discrimination in home rental and ownership.

amendment—a change made to a law or a legal document

Jim Crow segregation—laws and customs of racial exclusion to maintain white supremacy and racial discrimination

secede—to formally withdraw from a group or an organization, often to form another organization

Malcolm often rode along as Earl traveled to community meetings. He listened to Earl preach about honesty and hard work. But he also heard stories about injustices against the Black community. Church members spoke about being attacked by members of **hate groups** such as the Black Legion and the Ku Klux Klan (KKK). Some Black men were hunted and killed. Others were dragged from their homes in the night and beaten.

Hate Groups

The Ku Klux Klan was formed in 1866, and the Black Legion appeared in the 1930s. Both hate groups were started by people who believed that White people are superior to others because of skin color. They attacked Black families at night and used scare tactics to threaten those who didn't agree with them. Variations of the hate groups exist even today. The Southern Poverty Law Center is a civil rights organization that tracks hate groups. In 2018, it reported that there were 1,020 hate groups in the United States.

hate group—an organization that has beliefs and practices that attack an entire class of people based on things such as race, gender identity, or religion

Malcolm's father had witnessed hate because of his race. He had seen three of his six brothers killed by White people. Another brother would later be shot by white policemen. That hate showed up at his own doorstep too.

Just before Malcolm was born, the Little family was targeted by the Black Legion. The Black Legion disagreed with the things Earl preached. They felt Earl was spreading unrest among the Black community. Louise was home alone with Malcolm's three older siblings. The men broke all the windows in the home before leaving.

By the mid-1920s, the Ku Klux Klan had more than 4 million members. The hangman's noose became one of their main symbols of intimidation.

3 > EVERYTHING IN THE WORLD IS A HUSTLE

In an effort to give his family a fresh start, Earl bought 6 acres of land in Lansing, Michigan. Malcolm watched his father construct each part of their home.

Downtown Lansing, Michigan, in 1920. Malcolm lived in the Lansing area between 1928 and 1940.

Members of the Klan believed that having Black neighbors lowered their property values. A judge agreed, and when Malcolm was 4 years old, the Littles were forced to move. This wasn't enough for the Klan, though. Before Malcolm's family could go, two White men set fire to the home that Earl had worked so hard to finish. "The [W]hite police and firemen came and stood around watching as the house burned down to the ground," Malcolm remembered later.

One day in 1931, Earl left their new house in East Lansing to collect a debt from a neighbor. He never returned. Police officers found him badly beaten and run over by the wheels of a streetcar. Rumors spread that he had been attacked and then placed in front of the streetcar on purpose. Now, Louise and the children had to fend for themselves.

Louise was a Black woman new to town. She had eight children and a dead husband rumored to have been murdered. Earl's insurance company refused to pay the family what it was owed. They said Earl had killed himself, and the company did not cover suicide. Money became a problem.

Louise tried to make ends meet by working for White people. Those jobs would end when the employers realized that the light-skinned woman working for them was not White.

Then **welfare** workers began checking in on the family.

By 1940, 90 percent of jobs held by working women fell into 10 different categories, including nursing, teaching, and government work. However, Black women were usually only allowed to be domestic workers.

welfare—government aid in the form of money or necessities for those in need

The welfare workers had heard that Malcolm was stealing food. A neighbor told them he had offered the family free pork, but Louise had refused. They did not understand that eating pork was against Louise's religion. The neighbor and welfare workers felt that she should take what she could get.

In 1937, Louise was dragged screaming from her home. She was sent to a mental hospital in Kalamazoo, Michigan, about 70 miles (112.7 kilometers) away. She would remain there for the next 25 years. Her children, including 13-year-old Malcolm, were separated. At first, Malcolm lived with a friend's family. But his behavior problems at school would change that.

THE RACIAL UNITY MYTH

By 1939, racism and segregation against Black people had spread throughout the North. Despite that, Malcolm was sent to live with a White family in Mason, about 12 miles (19.3 km) away. The Swerlins made sure Malcolm ate well and had a room of his own. However, they would use **slurs** to describe him. They also made racist jokes to their friends. They did not seem to realize that their words hurt Malcolm.

Malcolm went to a White high school. He was intelligent and well-liked by his classmates. He joined the basketball team and was often asked to join other clubs and organizations. He always said yes.

slur—an insulting name or word

But he was still one of the only Black students. The history teacher was particularly fond of making racist jokes. When he traveled to basketball games, the other teams would call him names. His teammates and coaches didn't defend him. After the games, there would often be a school dance. Nobody danced with Malcolm.

One day, Malcolm's favorite teacher, Mr. Ostrowski, gave him some startling advice. Students were asked to think about their futures. They all said that Mr. Ostrowski had supported their dreams and ideas when they had shared them. But when the teacher met with Malcolm, his words were different. When Malcolm said he wanted to be a lawyer, Mr. Ostrowski grinned and shook his head. "A lawyer—that's no realistic goal for a n-----. You need to think about something you *can* be. . . . Why don't you plan on carpentry?"

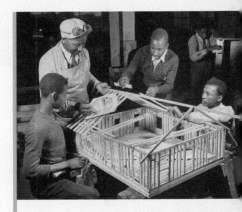

During the 1920s and 1930s, most jobs held by Black workers were either domestic or labor positions. Over the next two decades, this would change.

"It was then," Malcolm said, "that I began to change—inside."

Malcolm realized that, no matter what he achieved, White people would always see him differently. He wrote to his sister Ella, who lived in Boston, Massachusetts. She agreed to become his legal guardian.

Ella Mae Collins was 14 years older than Malcolm. She provided him with moral and financial support his entire life.

Life on the East Coast was exciting. Malcolm was attracted to the fast pace and flashy nightlife scene. He easily found friends and work. Ella arranged for him to work on a passenger train, serving sandwiches and entertaining passengers.

Malcolm's favorite part about the job was the layovers in Harlem, New York. He slicked his hair and wore fancy clothes. He answered to the name Detroit Red. He made money on the side as a **hustler**. It wasn't long before the local police learned his name.

Malcolm met a woman named Sophia. With a small group of friends, they planned robberies together. The police watched Malcolm's every move. One night they caught him with a stolen watch. Everyone was arrested. Sophia and her friend, both White women, were let go. Malcolm and his friend, Shorty, had their **bail** set at $10,000, an impossible amount for them to pay. In February 1946, Malcolm was sent to jail for 10 years. He wasn't even 21 years old.

bail—a sum of money paid to a court to allow someone accused of a crime to be set free until his or her trial

hustler—someone who does a job for extra money

Malcolm was sent to Charlestown State Prison in Boston, Massachusetts. The prison was more than 100 years old. Cells were cramped and without running water.

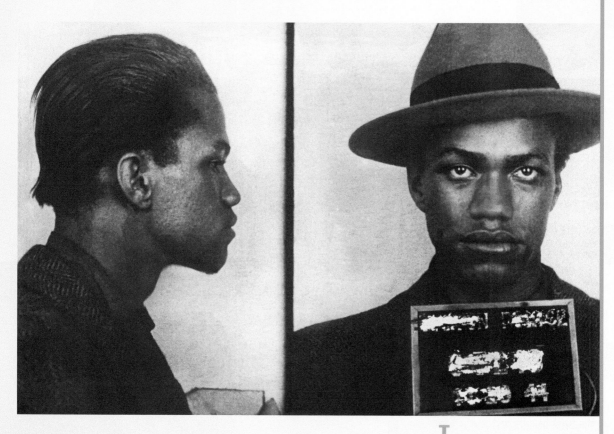

Malcolm's mug shot, 1944

The other inmates nicknamed Malcolm "Satan," because he was angry and mean when he arrived. He spent a lot of time locked up by himself. He transferred to other prisons. At Norfolk Prison Colony, Malcolm read as much as he could. The prison had a huge library, and inmates were allowed to select their own books. Educators from nearby colleges such as Harvard and Boston University came to the prison. They led lectures and debates that helped the prisoners expand their minds.

Then Malcolm's brother Reginald introduced him to the Nation of Islam.

The Other Side

The Nation of Islam (NOI) has received criticism for its **bigoted** teachings about White people, women, Jewish people, and gay people. Members of the NOI have also been accused of violence against others. Today the NOI is categorized as a hate group by the Southern Poverty Law Center. Its current leader, Louis Farrakhan, has not been allowed in the United Kingdom since 1986. He was banned from Facebook and Instagram in 2019 for spreading hate speech.

bigoted—an attitude of hatred or intolerance for members of a particular group

Malcolm wrote to Elijah Muhammad, the leader of the NOI. Muhammad wrote back. Elated, Malcolm began to read more about the NOI's teachings. He worked to **convert** other prisoners. He joined debates, perfecting his speaking skills. And in August 1952, he was released from prison.

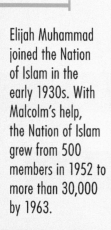

Elijah Muhammad joined the Nation of Islam in the early 1930s. With Malcolm's help, the Nation of Islam grew from 500 members in 1952 to more than 30,000 by 1963.

convert—to change from one religion or faith to another

Malcolm moved to Detroit, Michigan, with his brother Wilfred. Soon after, Malcolm finally met his mentor. Muhammad put Malcolm in charge of several NOI temples. He also sent Malcolm out to recruit young people. Malcolm traveled overseas to Africa to spread Muhammad's words. He spoke on radio and television programs. He even founded a successful newspaper, *Muhammad Speaks*. He wanted his followers to know that they had waited long enough for respect and human rights.

"My [B]lack brothers and sisters," Malcolm would say, "no one will ever know *who* we are . . . until we know who we are!" People would sit up and listen.

DID YOU KNOW?

In 1956, Malcolm met Betty Saunders, also known as Sister Betty X and, later, Betty Shabazz. They were married two years later. They had six daughters together.

Malcolm was admired and feared. He was a voice for change, and his following was undeniable. In early 1963, the *New York Times* named Malcolm as the second most sought-after speaker on college campuses. A **White supremacist** group offered a $10,000 **bounty** on him. Malcolm spoke out against injustice. But in 1963, speaking up put him at odds with his mentor.

Malcolm speaking at an outdoor rally in 1963

assassinate—to murder a person who is well-known or important

bounty—money offered for harming or killing someone or something

White supremacist—a person who believes that White people are superior to all others

Muhammad had been charged with inappropriate behavior by several women involved with the NOI. Such behavior went against the organization's teachings. Malcolm confronted his teacher, which angered Muhammad and many NOI leaders.

Then, on November 22, 1963, President John F. Kennedy was **assassinated**. When interviewed, Malcolm said that the hate in America had been responsible. His quote, "[Kennedy] never foresaw that chickens would come home to roost so soon," was read around the world. The NOI felt he was causing too much conflict. They silenced him for 90 days.

DID YOU KNOW?

In 1964, Malcolm started his own religious organization, Muslim Mosque, Inc. It was made up of mostly former NOI members.

Malcolm realized he needed a change. In 1964, he made his Hajj to Mecca. There, he met Muslims of all races. He realized his beliefs should evolve. "There were tens of thousands of pilgrims, from all over the world. They were of all colors, from blue-eyed blondes to black-skinned Africans. But we were all participating in the same ritual, displaying a spirit of unity and brotherhood that my experiences in America had led me to believe never could exist," he wrote later.

When Malcolm returned home, he started the Organization of Afro-American Unity (OAAU). A political group that incorporated his new beliefs, its members would fight for human rights of African Americans. They would also work toward cooperation between Africans and African Americans.

The NOI had not forgotten about Malcolm, though—and neither had the New York City police department or the Federal Bureau of Investigation (FBI). Both law enforcement groups had undercover agents shadowing Malcolm's every move.

On February 14, 1965, someone firebombed his home. Malcolm's family escaped, unharmed. But a week later, Malcolm gave a talk in the Audubon Ballroom in New York City. Two men stood up in the front row and fired at Malcolm as he stood unprotected on the stage. Other assassins shot him 15 times. Malcolm died on the way to the hospital. In the confusion, the shooters escaped, and only one man was caught at the scene. Later, three men who were members of the NOI were convicted—one confessed but said the others were innocent.

"It has always been my belief that I, too, will die by violence," Malcolm wrote in his autobiography. "I have done all that I can to be prepared."

Many wonder what Malcolm could have accomplished if he had survived. Movies, documentaries, and books have been produced about his life. Organizations have been created in his honor. People from around the world still visit his grave at the Ferncliff Cemetery in Hartsdale, New York, to pay their respects to the human and civil rights icon.

DID YOU KNOW?

The Autobiography of Malcolm X was published just a few months after Malcolm's death. It is still considered the most important book about his life.

GLOSSARY

activist (ak-TUH-vihst)—a person who works for social or political change

amendment (uh-MEND-muhnt)—a change made to a law or a legal document

assassinate (us-SASS-uh-nate)—to murder a person who is well-known or important

bail (BAYL)—a sum of money paid to a court to allow someone accused of a crime to be set free until his or her trial

bigoted (bih-GUHT-uhd)—an attitude of hatred or intolerance for members of a particular group

Black nationalism (BLACK NASH-uh-nuhl-iss-uhm)—the support or awareness for, and unity and independence of, black people in a country

bounty (BOUN-tee)—money offered for harming or killing someone or something

civil rights (SI-vil RYTS)—the rights that all people have to freedom and equal treatment under the law

convert (kuhn-VURT)—to change from one religion or faith to another

Hajj (HAHJ)—a religious journey to the holy city of Mecca, Saudi Arabia

hate group (HAYT GROOP)—an organization that has beliefs and practices that attack an entire class of people based on prejudices such as race, gender identity, or religion

human rights (HYOO-muhn RIGHTS)—the idea that all people should be treated fairly

hustler (HUHSS-luhr)—someone who does a job for extra money

Islam (ISS-luhm)—a religion founded on the Arabian Peninsula in the seventh century by the prophet Muhammad

Jim Crow segregation (JIM KROH seg-ruh-GAY-shuhn)—laws and customs of racial exclusion to maintain white supremacy and racial discrimination; Jim Crow laws were passed and upheld in the United States between 1877 to 1965

race leader (RAYS LEE-duhr)—an activist who unites people on the basis of shared racial, cultural, and historical beliefs; Marcus Garvey, W. E. B. Du Bois, and Malcolm X were some of the race leaders during the Civil Rights movement

secede (si-SEED)—to formally withdraw from a group or an organization, often to form another organization

slur (SLUR)—insulting name or word

welfare (WEL-fair)—government aid in the form of money or necessities for those in need

White supremacist (WHITE suh-PREH-muh-sust)—person who believes that White people are superior to all others.

READ MORE

Anderson, Carol. *We Are Not Yet Equal: Understanding Our Racial Divide.* New York: Bloomsbury, 2018.

Myers, Walter Dean. *Malcolm X: By Any Means Necessary: A Biography.* New York: Scholastic, 2019.

Smith-Llera, Danielle. *TV Exposes Brutality on the Selma March: 4D, An Augmented Reading Experience.* North Mankato, MN: Compass Point Books, 2020.

X, Malcolm, with Alex Haley. *The Autobiography of Malcolm X.* New York: Ballantine Books, 1965.

INTERNET SITES

The Civil Rights Movement
https://junior.scholastic.com/pages/content-hubs/the-civil-rights-movement.html

Malcolm X
http://www.MalcolmX.com

Southern Poverty Law Center
https://www.splcenter.org/

CRITICAL THINKING QUESTIONS

1. Malcolm's views and beliefs on how black people should work toward equality changed over the years. Find an event in his life and explain how it helped shift his opinion.

2. Malcolm had many mentors throughout his life. Choose one. How did that person shape his opinions?

3. Reread pages 10–11. Starting with the Civil War, turn the information you read into a timeline. Then add other world events. Do any timeline entries overlap those events? Do you think any overlapping events affected each other? Do any of the earlier events relate to later events?

INDEX